To Parents and Teachers:

We hope you and the children will enjoy reading this story in English and Spanish. It is simply told, but not *simplified,* so that both versions are quite natural. However, there is lots of repetition for practicing pronunciation, for helping develop memory skills, and for reinforcing comprehension.

At the back of the book, there is a simple picture dictionary with key words as well as a basic pronunciation guide to the whole story.

Here are a few suggestions for using the book:

• First, read the story aloud in English to become familiar with it. Treat it like any other picture book. Look at the drawings, talk about the story, the characters, and so on.

• Then look at the picture dictionary and repeat the key words in Spanish. Make this an active exercise. Ask the children to say the words out loud instead of reading them.

• Go back and read the story again, this time in English and Spanish. Don't worry if your pronunciation isn't quite correct. Just have fun trying it out. If necessary, check the guide at the back of the book, but you'll soon pick up how to say the Spanish words.

• When you think you and the children are ready, try reading the story in Spanish. Ask the children to say it with you. Only ask them to read it if they seem eager to try. The spelling could be confusing and discourage them.

• Above all, encourage the children, and give them lots of praise. They are usually quite unselfconscious, so let them be children and playact, try different voices, and have fun. This is an excellent way to build confidence for acquiring foreign language skills.

**First paperback edition for the United States, its Dependencies, Canada
and the Philippines published 1998 by Barron's Educational Series, Inc.
Text © Copyright 1998 by b small publishing, Surrey, England.**

International Standard Book Number 0-7641-5129-0   Library of Congress Catalog Card Number 98-72554
Printed in Hong Kong   9 8 7 6 5 4 3

Get dressed, Robbie

Vístete, Robertito

Lone Morton

Pictures by Anna C. Leplar
Spanish by Rosa Martín

BARRON'S

Every morning, Robbie's mom lays out clothes for him to get dressed.

Todas las mañanas, la mamá de Robertito le prepara la ropa para que se vista.

But some mornings Robbie likes to choose his own clothes.

Pero algunas mañanas Robertito prefiere elegir su ropa él solo.

Sometimes Robbie puts on clothes
that are too big,

A veces Robertito se pone ropa que
es demasiado grande,

sometimes clothes that are too small.

a veces ropa que es demasiado pequeña.

Sometimes Robbie puts on winter clothes,

A veces Robertito se pone ropa de invierno,

sometimes summer clothes.

a veces ropa de verano.

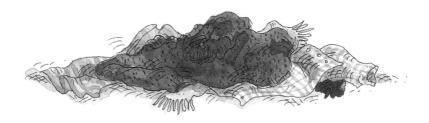

And sometimes he puts on clothes
from his dressing-up box!

¡Y a veces se pone ropa de su cajón
de disfraces!

But today, Robbie puts on his green, spotty T-shirt,

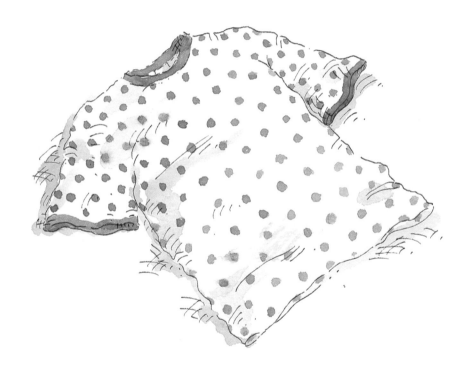

Pero hoy, Robertito se pone su camiseta verde de lunares,

his patterned shorts,

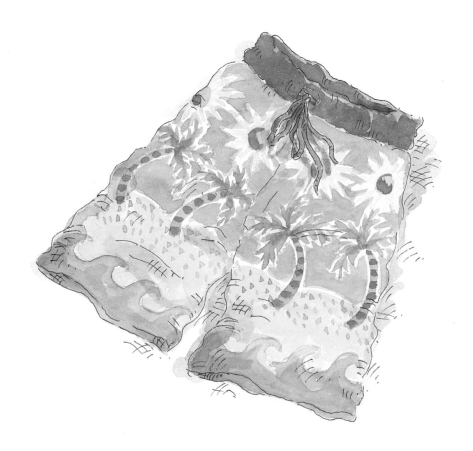

sus pantalones cortos estampados,

one orange sock,
un calcetín anaranjado,

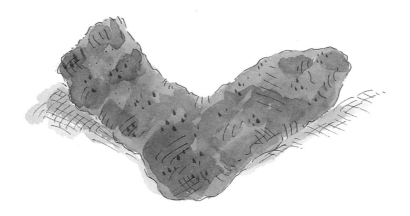

one striped sock,
un calcetín de rayas,

one blue plastic sandal,
una sandalia azul de plástico,

one crocodile slipper,
una zapatilla en forma de cocodrilo,

his pink baseball cap,
su gorra de béisbol rosa,

a very long, checked scarf,
una bufanda de cuadros muy larga,

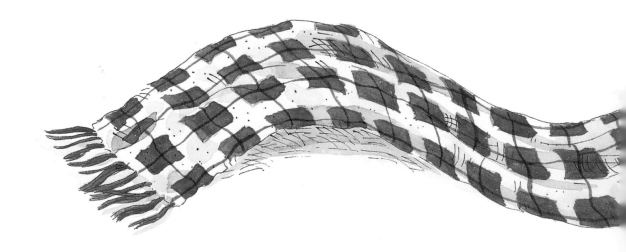

a pair of sunglasses,
unas gafas de sol,

a necklace of wooden beads,
un collar de bolitas de madera,

and his brand-new backpack, with his favorite car and ten color crayons.

y su mochila nueva, con su coche favorito y diez gises de colores.

"Robbie, we have to go out!"
calls Mom. "Are you dressed yet?"

—¡Robertito, tenemos que irnos!—
llama mamá. —¿Ya estás vestido?—

"Yes," says Robbie, "I am dressed.
I'm going to
wear this…!"

—Sí,—dice Robertito.—Ya estoy vestido.
¡Voy a llevar
esto…!—

Pronouncing Spanish

Don't worry if your pronunciation isn't quite correct. The important thing is to be willing to try. The pronunciation guide here is based on the Spanish accent used in Latin America. Although it cannot be completely accurate, it certainly will be a great help.

• Read the guide as naturally as possible, as if it were English.

• Put stress on the letters in *italics,* e.g. *roh*-pah.

If you can, ask a Spanish-speaking person to help and move on as soon as possible to speaking the words without the guide.

Note: Spanish adjectives usually have two forms, one for masculine and one for feminine nouns. They often look very similar but are pronounced slightly differently, e.g. **pequeña** and **pequeño** (see below).

Words Las palabras

lass pal-*abrass*

clothes
la ropa

lah *roh*-pah

T-shirt
la camiseta

lah kahmee-*seh*-tah

big
grande

grahn-deh

small
pequeño/pequeña

peh-*kehn*-yoh/peh-*kehn*-yah

shorts
los pantalones cortos
loss pantah-*loh*-ness *kor*-toss

sandals
las sandalias
lass san*dal*-eeass

backpack
la mochila
lah moch*ee*-lah

scarf
la bufanda
lah boo*fan*-dah

slipper
la zapatilla
lah sapa*tee*-ya

sunglasses
las gafas de sol
lass *gah*-fass deh sol

socks
los calcetines
lohs kahl-seh-*tee*-nehs

car
el coche
el *koh*-cheh

green
verde

vair-deh

orange
anaranjado/a

ahn-aran-hah-doh/dah

blue
azul

ah-sool

pink
rosa

roh-sah

crayons
los gises de colores

loss hee-sess deh koh-loh-ress

necklace
el collar

el koh-yahr

winter
el invierno

el eenvee-air-noh

cap
la gorra

lah gor-rah

summer
el verano

el vair-ah-noh

striped
de rayas

deh rah-yass

spotty
de lunares

deh loonar-ess

checked
de cuadros

deh kwah-dross

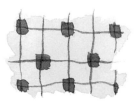

patterned
estampado/a

esstampah-doh/dah

A simple guide to pronouncing this Spanish story

Vístete, Robertito
*vee*stet-teh, rober*tee*-toh

Todas las mañanas, la mamá de Robertito
*to*dass lass man-*yah*-nass, lah mam*ma* deh rober*tee*-toh

le prepara la ropa
leh preh-*pah*-rah lah *roh*-pah

para que se vista.
*pa*rah keh seh *vee*stah

Pero algunas mañanas Robertito prefiere elegir su ropa él solo.
pair-roh al*goo*-nass man-*yah*-nass rober*tee*-toh pref-ee-*air*-eh eleh-*heer* soo *roh*-pah el *soh*-loh

A veces Robertito se pone ropa que es demasiado grande,
ah *veh*-sees rober*tee*-toh seh *poh*-neh *roh*-pah keh ess demass-*yah*-doh *gran*-deh

a veces ropa que es demasiado pequeña.
ah *veh*-sess *roh*-pah keh ess demass-*yah*-doh peh-*kehn*-yah

A veces Robertito se pone ropa de invierno,
ah *veh*-sess rober*tee*-toh seh *poh*-neh *roh*-pah deh ennvee-*air*-noh

a veces ropa de verano.
ah *veh*-sess *roh*-pah deh vair-*ah*-noh

¡Y a veces se pone ropa de su cajón de disfraces!
ee ah *veh*-sess seh *poh*-neh *roh*-pah deh soo cah-*hon* deh dees-*fras*-sess

Pero hoy, Robertito se pone su camiseta verde de lunares,
pair-roh oy rober*tee*-toh seh *poh*-neh soo kah-mee-*seh*-tah *vair*-deh deh loonar-ess

sus pantalones cortos estampados,
soos pantah-*loh*-ness *kor*-toss esstam*pah*-doss

un calcetín anaranjado,
oon kahl-seh-*teen* ahn-aran-*hah*-doh

un calcetín de rayas,
oon kahl-seh-*teen* deh *rah*-yass

una sandalia azul, de plástico,
*oo*nah san*dal*-eeah ah-*sool*, deh *plas*teekoh

una zapatilla en forma de cocodrilo,
*oo*nah sapa*tee*-ya en *for*mah deh koko-*dree*-loh

su gorra de béisbol rosa,
soo *gor*-rah deh baseball *roh*-sah

una bufanda de cuadros muy larga,
*oo*nah boo-*fan*-dah deh *kwa*-dross mwee *lahr*-gah

unas gafas de sol,
*oo*nass *gah*-fass deh sol

un collar de bolitas de madera,
oon koh-*yahr* deh bol-*eet*-ass deh ma*deh*-rah

y su mochila nueva, con su coche favorito y diez gises de colores.
ee soo moch*ee*-lah noo*oeh*-vah kon soo *koh*-cheh favor-*ee*-toh ee dee-*ess* *hee*-sess deh koh-*loh*-ress

—¡Robertito, tenemos que irnos!— llama mamá.—¿Ya estás vestido?—
rober*tee*-toh, tenem-oss keh *eer*-noss *yah*-mah mam*ma*, ya ess-*tass* ves-*tee*-doh

—Si,—dice, Robertito.—Ya estoy vestido. ¡Voy a llevar esto…!—
see, *dee*-seh rober*tee*-toh, ya ess-*toy* ves-*tee*-doh, voy ah yeh-*var* ess-toh